Osann . Mayer . Wiele
The Design Thinking Quick Start Guide

ISABELL OSANN · LENA MAYER · INGA WIELE

THE DESIGN THINKING QUICK START GUIDE

A 6-STEP PROCESS FOR GENERATING AND IMPLEMENTING CREATIVE SOLUTIONS

- TEAM TOOLS AND ACTIVITIES
- CHECKLISTS
- SAMPLE WORKSHOP AGENDAS

WILEY

For general information on our other products and services or for technical support, please contact our Customer Care Department within the United States at (800) 762-2974, outside the United States at (317) 572-3993 or fax (317) 572-4002.

Wiley publishes in a variety of print and electronic formats and by print-on-demand. Some material included with standard print versions of this book may not be included in e-books or in print-on-demand. If this book refers to media such as a CD or DVD that is not included in the version you purchased, you may download this material at http://booksupport.wiley.com. For more information about Wiley products, visit www.wiley.com.

Library of Congress Cataloging-in-Publication Data:
Names: Osann, Isabell, author. | Mayer, Lena, author. | Wiele, Inga, author.
Title: The design thinking quick start guide : a 6-step process for generating and implementing creative solutions / Isabell Osann, Lena Mayer, Inga Wiele.
Other titles: Design Thinking Schnellstart. English
Description: Hoboken, New Jersey : John Wiley & Sons, [2020]
Identifiers: LCCN 2019050493 (print) | LCCN 2019050494 (ebook) | ISBN 9781119679899 (paperback) | ISBN 9781119679875 (adobe pdf) | ISBN 9781119679882 (epub)
Subjects: LCSH: Product design. | Creative thinking. | Brainstorming. | Group problem solving.
Classification: LCC TS171.4 .O8313 2020 (print) | LCC TS171.4 (ebook) | DDC 658.5/752—dc23
LC record available at https://lccn.loc.gov/2019050493
LC ebook record available at https://lccn.loc.gov/2019050494

Illustrations: Inga Wiele, Dreamland GmbH & Co. KG
Design: Dreamland GmbH & Co. KG
Translated by: Amy Buer

Printed in the United States of America

V10016443_122019

CONTENTS

WHAT TO EXPECT

This workbook will help you apply Design Thinking to your challenges and projects. It will help you generate ideas for new products, services or business models. It will also help you adopt solutions in manageably small increments. With checklists and descriptions for each phase of the Design Thinking process, you will be able to design a creative workshop for your colleagues and team members.

We are grateful for questions and feedback on our book and we look forward to hearing from you. May your Design Thinking workshops be creative and inspiring!

TOOL KIT
LEARNING JOURNAL
CHECKLIST
SAMPLE AGENDAS
WORKSHOP MATERIALS

DESIGN THINKING IN SIX PHASES

Build empathy to understand the user or the customer.

View the world from different perspectives.

Think of as many ideas as possible

Make the ideas understandable.

phase two
Observe

phase four
Ideate

phase five
Prototype

ORIENTATION

SOLUTION

phase one
Understand

phase three
Synthesize

phase six
Test

Is there a common understanding of the problem? Does your team understand different perspectives of the issue at hand?

Which needs should be met?

Test with users or customers and deliver what is required.

HOW DO I USE THIS BOOK?

HOW SHOULD I USE THIS BOOK?

A. What is the purpose of this book?

This book offers the hands-on information you need to use Design Thinking to develop innovative solutions in your work environment. It is also a guide for people who already have experience and would like to learn new methods and new ways of using Design Thinking in their work.

START FAST

KEEP IT SIMPLE

We encourage you to try out different methods and tools from the book. For each of the six phases of Design Thinking, we have included an introduction followed by tools and activities. This structure will allow you to guide others through working with Design Thinking.

During this process, we would like to encourage you to reflect on what you have learned and experienced in the individual phases. On some pages, you will find space to write down your thoughts about what worked well, and what you would like to try to do differently the next time.

This book is the result of our joint Design Thinking workshops from 2016 to 2019 and combines expertise from industry practice and teaching in a university context.

CONCRETE GUIDANCE

FOCUS ON WHAT'S ESSENTIAL

This is a practical guide for real-world use. We have included tips for further reading, for those who would like to understand the methods in greater detail.

B. How is this book structured?
The following chapter offers a brief introduction to the topic of creativity, and Chapter III explains the concept of a "Design Challenge" and includes two useful activities.

The main part of the book (Chapters 01 to 06) will guide you through the six phases of the Design Thinking process. At the beginning of each phase, two warm-ups are presented to help teams adjust to the style of working in that phase. Some phases are more challenging in terms of teamwork. For these phases, we offer you additional explanations so that the process steps are smoother and easier to complete.

The important concept of "iteration" and tools for documenting work are explained in Chapter IV. Additional information on warm-ups, teamwork, and two sample agendas – one-day or two-day – will complete the book (Chapters V and VI).

STRUCTURE

Goal: What is the method/tool for?

Preparation: Previous steps

Procedure: Detailed description of the individual steps

Individual Steps and Procedures

Reflection

WARM-UP

METHODS AND TOOLS

🏳 --------------------

🧊 --------------------

➚ --------------------

📖 --------------------

🕐 **Duration and number of participants in the warm-up**

❓ **Sample questions, mindset**

🔖 **Materials**

⚲ **Variations**

📖 **Reference to** further reading, literature and/or supplementary methods, sources

Reflection: In each phase, this area offers you space to record your experience. Here you can write down insights, ideas, process steps, attitudes, etc. from each phase for the next run-through or transfer these concepts into your work or personal life.

⚑ **Goal of the phase**

⤷ **Phase Procedure**

☑ **Checklist**

PHASES

⚑ --

⤷ --

☑ --

REFLECTION ...

📖 ----------------------------------

📖 **Phase Checklists are inspired by "the unpublished Workshop Guide" Menning, Y. (2015):** The Idea Gym – training the design thinking muscle.

📖 **Reference to** further reading, literature, and/or supplementary methods, sources

WHAT'S ALL THIS ABOUT CREATIVITY?

II

WHERE DOES CREATIVITY COME FROM?

By creativity we mean an attitude that aims to discover and create something new, a willingness to experiment and to venture into unknown territory. A creative mindset is key for innovation. To develop creative solutions in a new environment, it is important to value the ideas of others, while also having faith in your own abilities. Confidence in being able to bring about change creatively can be trained like a muscle (cf. Kelley/Kelley, 2013, pp. 2, 9).

Innovations often originate when different fields merge, where people with different backgrounds and attitudes must work together. However, the ultimate value of a solution is not decided by the team, but rather the user or customer. They are like the "sun" of the innovation process. Everything revolves around their problems, wishes, and needs.

That's why the best people to ask for new ideas are the customers. Using the Design Thinking method, you will be able to focus on your (potential) customers and create solutions that fit their needs.

Ideas for new products, services, and business models can be quickly developed as well as ideas for a successful implementation. This "agile" approach offers more than just a tool kit and results. There is also a supporting philosophy and space for creativity. A flexible physical workspace as well as the team culture (mutual respect, trust, seeing failure as useful, constructive feedback) are essential for success.

Kelley, T./Kelley, D. (2013): *Creative Confidence.* New York: Crown Business.

The British comedian John Cleese explains in his lecture different conditions that encourage creative thinking.

SPACE (PHYSICAL AND MENTAL)

TIME (LIMITED)

TIME (UNLIMITED)

CREATIVE CONFIDENCE

HUMOR

SPACE (PHYSICAL AND MENTAL)

Two basic methods of thinking are a) concentration (or closed mode), and b) release (or open mode). It is recommended to concentrate on a problem for a limited period of time in "closed mode" and then to wait for inspiration in "open mode" indefinitely – without putting a narrow time frame on things.

Inspiring spaces filled with possibilities create good environments for creative thinking.

CONCENTRATION

RELEASE

 Source: https://www.wissenschaft.de/umwelt-natur/die-wissenschaft-vom-musenkuss/ (GER) ● **Cleese, J. on Creativity:** https://www.youtube.com/watch?v=Pb5oIIPO62g

19

1 Preparatory phase (awareness raising)
Creative thinking starts when information is gathered in the mind, problems are defined, interests are considered or a rough goal is explained. This phase typically takes place for a limited time, with concentrated work (focused, closed state).

TIME (LIMITED)

2 Incubation phase
At some point, a possible answer to the previously discovered problems is unconsciously found. This is called "divergent thinking" and it is mostly an unconscious process. This type of thinking is characterized by alpha waves in the brain.
Cleese describes one's typical subjective feeling of having "unlimited" time in this "open" state.

TIME (UNLIMITED)

3 Illumination
The "AHA!" experience is the moment when there is a "click" in your brain. It's the moment when a new solution suddenly reveals itself.

4 Verification
Next, ideas that could solve the problem are tested and the solution is further developed or ruled out through feedback and additional iterations.

TIME (LIMITED)

Even though it is critical for creativity, people often do not consider the incubation phase when planning projects. When generating solutions, most teams prefer quick successes and creativity at the push of a button. The good news is that Design Thinking tools usually help teams get off to a great start, through changes in perspective, diverse teams, and improved customer understanding. Nevertheless, it has been proven that really good ideas take time to mature. Our advice: Stay in the loop and organize shorter Design Thinking sessions more often, which are interrupted by a few days away from direct work on the problem. Time will make a worthy contribution to the creative process.

 ● **Csikszentmihalyi, M. (2013):** *Creativity: Flow and the Psychology of Discovery and Invention.* Harper Perennial Modern Classics.

CREATIVE CONFIDENCE

David Kelley, co-founder of Design Thinking and founder of the design firm IDEO, defined the term "creative confidence."

Creative confidence is trust in one's own creative potential to reshape the world. In order to achieve good results, the entire team needs to be able to share this confidence with each other. It is much like a tightrope act. Each individual member of a team must believe they can stand on the rope and move forward. And while moving forward they must be sure that the other members of the team will support them and catch them, if needed. Attention and appreciation are the rewards for those willing to work outside of a safe environment and take responsibility to ensure the emotional safety of others.

Acknowledging these rewards strengthens the creative confidence in a team. And the positive spiral begins again. Teams and individuals naturally learn creative confidence through the regular use of Design Thinking tools and concepts.

SUPPORTIVE CONDITIONS FOR CREATIVE THINKING 4/4

Additionally, in everyday life, we can repeatedly observe our own attitudes toward problem-solving situations to train our creative confidence:

- Try experiencing a few minutes of "unbounded" attention every day (e.g. looking out the window while traveling on public transport, or looking at the surroundings while waiting for something). The freedom of moving thoughts – spiritual meandering (cf. Csikszentmihalyi, M., 2015, p. 147) – supports your abilities to handle new ideas.
- Treat yourself to breaks during work. Defocusing creates space for new neuronal connections to form.
- Question it. How does something fit into the world? Why doesn't it fit? What is the essence? Nothing is isolated.
- Use alternative and less familiar travel routes in everyday life. There's a lot to observe.
- Foster your underdeveloped talents.
- Be willing to experiment and gain confidence with small, creative tasks.
- Have the courage to fail.
- Perform a quick and imperfect start instead of an elegant hesitation.

HUMOR

- Humor is a central component of spontaneity.
- Humor makes it easier for you to get started in an open and creative working attitude.
- Fail hilariously and then iterate.

In our workshops, we often experience how difficult it is for people to move from thinking to doing and simply MAKING something. However, when they start, most are pleasantly surprised by a "flow feeling" that makes creative ideas appear to emerge out of nowhere.

 Source: http://www.designkit.org/mindsets; https://rework.withgoogle.com/blog/five-keys-to-a-successful-google-team/

DO IT!

ITERATE

LEARN FROM
MISTAKES!

III

WHAT IS A DESIGN CHALLENGE?

CREATING DESIGN CHALLENGES

At the beginning of the team/project work, the team defines a question or a starting topic, which is called a "Design Challenge" in Design Thinking. When the individual phases are run through several times, the Design Challenge is adapted and refined again and again.

It is important to keep in mind that the Design Challenge …

- … is defined in such a way that people can be interviewed or observed. A good Design Challenge is about designing an experience for someone else – not for yourself!
- … does not yet contain any solutions or restrictions (e.g. NOT "… reduce costs")

The following wording helps to define the situation:
"Rethink/Redesign the [topic] experience." or "Rethink/Redesign [topic] experience for [specific users]."

Design Challenge Examples

- Rethink the disposal of packaging waste, considering the widespread use of Amazon, etc.
- Redesign the customer experience in local public transport.

Collect all the information for your Design Challenge together in a group, e.g. via a mindmap or with another tool on a whiteboard.

Why?	$\rightarrow$	problem
Who?	$\rightarrow$	(potential) users
What?	$\rightarrow$	aims
With what?	$\rightarrow$	available resources
Who/What else?	$\rightarrow$	competition, alternatives

 CHECKLIST for the specification of the Design Challenge
- ○ Which activities should be carried out or supported for your user/customer?
- ○ What would you like to learn about the user/customer?
- ○ What solutions are already available? What's missing?
- ○ What does each step of the entire customer experience look like?
- ○ Who should be involved? Who are the stakeholders?

DEFINE THE INITIAL QUESTION AND "QUESTION THE QUESTION"

 Ensure a common understanding of the task within the group. Required time approx. 20 minutes.

 Formulate the initial question/initial Design Challenge.

 1 Silent writing (three minutes): Each participant writes down the aspects and questions on Post-its that come into their minds. One topic per Post-it!

2 All participants gather in front of a wall. One after another, they all read their points out loud and stick them unstructured to the wall (the other participants do not offer any comments yet).

3 Afterward, all participants are asked to arrange the Post-its thematically in silence. The same Post-it can be moved several times.

4 Finally, speaking is allowed again. In the team, the participants name the clusters that have emerged. After naming the clusters, whether all the team members are in agreement with the chosen categories will be discussed. Perhaps more sorting is required.

5 The open topics (relevant to the question) are sorted according to importance or into a meaningful sequence.

6 The person who initiated the project or the initial question should answer any open questions.

7 The topics that are automatically included in the process should be discussed and clarified (e.g. who is the customer, stakeholder, ...)

8 If necessary, the question can be reformulated as a "team question" (see next page).

"GET CONSENSUS ON THE QUESTION"

 Formulate a common team question based on the initial question. Required time approx. 15 minutes.

 Formulate initial question, "question the question."

1 Silent writing (three minutes): Each participant writes a new question on a Post-it. The new question describes her/his personal understanding of the original question.

2 All participants gather in front of a wall. One after another, they read their questions aloud and stick them to the wall.

3 The participants then discuss whether a question already represents a common understanding.

4 If there are no clear favorites, the keywords of the questions are underlined.

5 Each keyword is written on a new Post-it.

6 The participants put the keywords in a sequence so that a meaningful sentence can be created.

7 The sentence is written on a sheet of paper, so it is visible to everyone. A vote is held to determine if all team members agree with it, or not.

① Write

② Collect

③ Quietly cluster

④ Prioritize

"There is only one boss:
the customer.
And he can fire everybody in the
company, from the chairman on
down, simply by spending his
money somewhere else."

Sam Walton

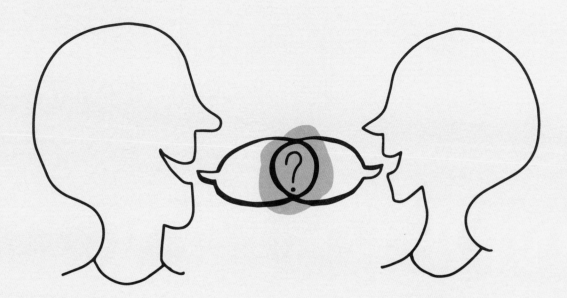

01 UNDERSTAND

MAP YOURSELVES

The participants distribute themselves throughout the room.

- The moderator asks a question and asks all participants to group themselves according to their answers. Like, "What's the last thing you did before you went to bed last night?" or "Which digital communication technology do you particularly like to use?"
- Several different question rounds can take place at your discretion. You can move from general to specific and ask questions to get everyone in the mood for teamwork. If, for example, the Design Challenge is about the development of a marketing strategy, a possible final question of this warm-up could be "Which brand had the last marketing campaign that you remember as being very positive?"

Reflection

This warm-up serves to reflect the attitudes, interests, and needs of all participants. You will learn a lot about your group members within a short time. It helps to see which answers participants give and how. This is also the first step in the Understand phase, where opinions, knowledge, associations, and experiences are shared regarding the Design Challenge. The aim is to find out what knowledge already exists in the team and which questions they have about the topic.

 12 min

 Sample questions:
What is your first drink in the morning? • What sport did you follow in your youth? • What time do you get up on workdays? • What brand is your current smartphone? • Which app do you use the most?

1 TRUTH & 1 LIE

This warm-up is an alternative to a classic introductory round and goes as follows: The participants stand in a circle or sit in the room so they can see each other.

- Everyone introduces themselves, one after the other, with two facts from their lives. One fact is true, the other is invented (for example, a wish). It is easiest if the workshop moderator starts the round, for example, A) "I live with my family in a detached house on the North Sea and we share our home with 18 pets." B) "In 2004 I was a runner-up in the curling world championship."
- After each person, the moderator asks the participants to vote by a show of hands: "Who believes that fact A is truth? I see. And who believes that fact B is a lie?"
- Each participant then reveals the truth with a short comment about the story.

Reflection

This warm-up serves to reflect on the interests and stories of all the participants. In a playful way, one learns new and sometimes surprising things about the group members. The warm-up relaxes the atmosphere in the room, especially for participants who have never met before. And new, previously unknown stories can also be discovered between colleagues of many years.

approx. 1–2 min per participant

Variations:
With more time: 2 truths & 1 lie.
With little time and large groups: Form teams of five or six people (best grouped according to the future Design Challenge teams).

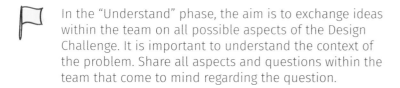

PHASE
UNDERSTAND

 In the "Understand" phase, the aim is to exchange ideas within the team on all possible aspects of the Design Challenge. It is important to understand the context of the problem. Share all aspects and questions within the team that come to mind regarding the question.

You have about 30 minutes to get through the challenge and determine: "What do we already know as a team?" and "What don't we know yet?" Collect all of this information as a team in a mindmap on a whiteboard (alternative methods: charette, semantic analysis).

 1 Share your experience
- ○ Assumptions
- ○ Opinions
- ○ Ideas
- ○ Stories
- ○ Associations

2 Examine the challenge
- ○ What are the building blocks of the challenge?
- ○ Who might be affected? (stakeholders)

3 Organize collected data, group information, and name the clusters

4 Define fields of interest and prepare for field research
- ○ Go through all the categories again.
- ○ Formulate questions for field research.
- ○ Define roles (interviewer, note taker, etc.).

REFLECTION ...

Smith, K. (2008): *How to Be an Explorer of the World: Portable Life Museum*. New York: Penguin Books.

UNDERSTANDING WITH THE CHARETTE METHOD

Identify some of the first relevant information in the team about users or customers. This method is well suited if you are working with several different user groups or if you have not yet identified your potential user groups. For your first brainstorming activity, we suggest the following structure:

Possible structure of a whiteboard:
1 Potential users (groups)
2 Assumptions about their needs or tasks
3 Which topics or ideas are hidden within the larger topic? As you share assumptions about your customer or user groups within the team, you will discover areas where you need to find out more. These findings will then flow into the preparation of the next phase: "Observe."

WHAT?
- Identify user groups for later field research, perhaps similar situations, and to determine user cases for the future solution.
- Anticipate needs and issues for possible interviews and observation questions.

WHO ARE POTENTIAL USERS?

WHAT NEEDS DO THEY HAVE?

WHAT IDEAS ARE HIDDEN?

Charette – in English: "the cart" – denotes a method of joint, open, and public planning. The basic metaphor is the joint drawing of the symbol of the cart. The method is used for different forms of public participation, cf. Deutsches Architektenblatt: https://www.dabonline.de/2008/02/01/ein-karren-fur-alle/ (GER)

Brainstorming first relevant user or customer information with the Charette Method

"Embrace what you don't know, especially in the beginning, because what you don't know can become your greatest asset.
It ensures that you will absolutely be doing things different from everybody else."

Sara Blakely

02

OBSERVE

ROLE SWAP

All participants should find a partner.

Round 1
Partner A interviews partner B on a specific topic. After three minutes, partner B changes and interviews partner A on the same topic (also for three minutes). Pairs are advised at the beginning that it is important to listen carefully to their counterparts as they will share the information gathered from the partner's point of view in the next round. Possible interview topics are, for example, "What did you do the past weekend?" or "What do you enjoy doing in your free time?"

Round 2
Each participant finds a new partner in the room. The topic of the interview remains the same and so does the duration of the interviews (2 x 3 minutes). But now, as an interviewee, each person takes on the role of the previous partner and answers from their point of view. This means that when Partner C interviews Partner A, he or she is responding from Partner B's point of view. Pretend to be the first person you interviewed. Do not use statements such as, "so partner B would probably say ..."

Reflection
The warm-up serves to build empathy with another person quickly. Participants practice listening. This is good preparation for surveys and observations in field research. Field research will focus on thinking and putting oneself in the situation, environment, perspective, and needs of (potential) users.

2 x 3 min per question

Sample questions for the interview:
How would you create a perfect day for yourself? ● How do you deal with new technologies? ● What is a good mobility concept for a city?

BLIND PORTRAIT

Two people talk to each other, and at the same time, draw a portrait of the other person without looking at the sheet of paper. Partners have two minutes for this activity.

Simple topics are suitable for discussion, such as:

- What is your name and your role in the company/ project? (This is appropriate if the participants do not know each other very well yet.)
- How did you get here this morning?
- What did you have for breakfast?
  (The moderator suggests a topic for discussion.)

It is important to explain to the participants beforehand that the exercise is not about drawing as realistically as possible. The results turn out best if you don't look at the sheet of paper.

You can very quickly see from the results who has drawn blindly and who has not. It's not about drawing a lifelike picture.

Each "artist" then writes the name of their model on the sheet and briefly introduces the person to the other participants on the basis of the drawing. If the participants agree, tape the pictures to a wall so everyone can see them.

Reflection
The exercise has a very energizing effect, with a lot of laughter and a developing sense of community. It fosters the ability to "let go," and participants are often surprised at how artistic the pictures seem when they have been drawn without looking. In this exercise, the brain works at full speed.

approx. 5 min

Material:
one sheet of paper and one felt-tip pen per participant

41

PHASE
OBSERVE

The "Observe" phase is about finding new ideas and as much information as possible about the problem and the potential users. You will want to capture and better understand needs, actions, thoughts, motivations, and behaviors for the Design Challenge. Focus on listening and observing. Avoid making assumptions and judgments during this phase.

You have about 15 minutes to prepare interview questions for field research and about 45 minutes to interview two to three potential users.

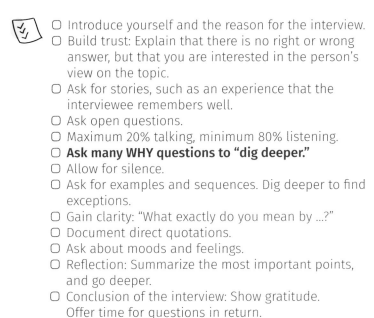

- ○ Introduce yourself and the reason for the interview.
- ○ Build trust: Explain that there is no right or wrong answer, but that you are interested in the person's view on the topic.
- ○ Ask for stories, such as an experience that the interviewee remembers well.
- ○ Ask open questions.
- ○ Maximum 20% talking, minimum 80% listening.
- ○ **Ask many WHY questions to "dig deeper."**
- ○ Allow for silence.
- ○ Ask for examples and sequences. Dig deeper to find exceptions.
- ○ Gain clarity: "What exactly do you mean by ...?"
- ○ Document direct quotations.
- ○ Ask about moods and feelings.
- ○ Reflection: Summarize the most important points, and go deeper.
- ○ Conclusion of the interview: Show gratitude. Offer time for questions in return.

REFLECTION ...

Nichols, R. G. & Stevens, L.A. (1957): *Are You Listening?* New York: McGraw-Hill. ● **Robertson, A. (1994):** *Listen for Success,* Burr Ridge: Irwin Professional Publishing. ● **Barker, L. & Watson, K. (2000):** *Listen Up: How to Improve Relationships, Reduce Stress, and Be More Productive by Using the Power of Listening,* New York: St. Martin's Press ● **Taheri, von Schmieden & Mayer, online course:** https://open.hpi.de/courses/insights-2017

CONDUCT QUALITATIVE INTERVIEWS

Interview Tips

- Team roles: an interviewer, a note taker
- Ask for the reason ⟶ Why?
- Make time for stories
- Ask open questions
- Formulate one-dimensional and clear questions
- Wait patiently during silent pauses
- Avoid passing judgment
- Pay attention to your body language
- 20:80 (interviewer:interviewee)

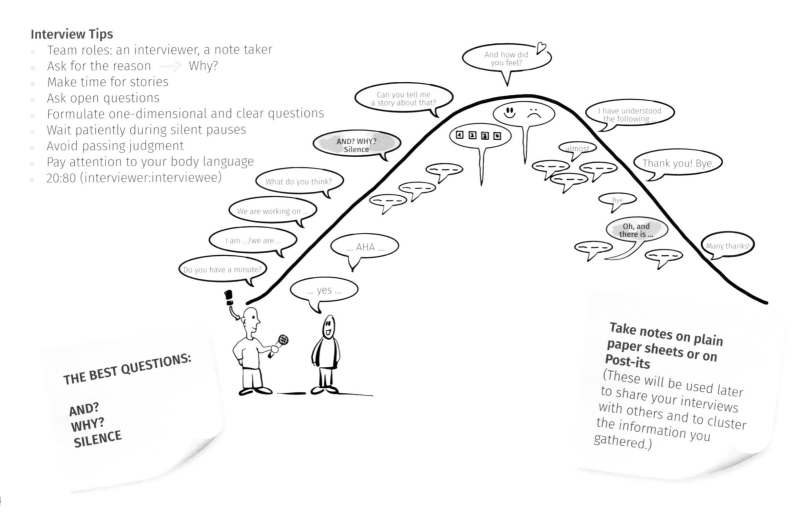

THE BEST QUESTIONS:

AND?
WHY?
SILENCE

Take notes on plain paper sheets or on Post-its
(These will be used later to share your interviews with others and to cluster the information you gathered.)

FROM OBSERVE TO SYNTHESIZE

 Remove yourself from your everyday life and get into the world of the user! After every conversation and every observation, reflect on what you have seen and heard, as well as your own behavior. Also, consider what you can improve in follow-up interviews or observations. You can use various tools to structure your observations: e.g. empathy maps.

 CHECKLIST for the Structure
- ○ Who are the users?
- ○ What do the users do?
- ○ Who influences the users or is in contact with them?
- ○ How do the users differ from one another?
- ○ What's the situation?
- ○ What needs exist?

 Take a few minutes for reflection after each interview. The following questions might help you.

CHECKLIST for Reflection
- ○ Was there an AHA moment, contradictions, something that surprised you?
- ○ Is there a need worth fulfilling?
- ○ Did your questioning techniques work well?
- ○ Is your documentation helpful?
- ○ Are there things you want to stop or do differently for the next observation?
- ○ Is there something you want to focus on during future observations?

 Lewrick, M. et al. (2017): *The Design Thinking Playbook.* München: Vahlen (GER) ● **Lewrick, M. et al. (2017):** AEIOU Framework (p. 21), Jobs-to-be-done Framework (p. 55).

"If I have seen further than others,
it is by standing upon the
shoulders of giants."

Isaac Newton

03

SYNTHESIZE

HOW TO MAKE TOAST

All participants need a piece of paper and a pencil.

Have participants silently visualize and draw how they make toast (three minutes). Then view and discuss the drawings together: What is the focus of the drawing? What is included in the preparation process? (Does someone start baking the bread?) Or in the purchasing process? Or with the kitchen appliances?

Reflection

The warm-up is intended to introduce the convergent mindset of the "Synthesize" phase. Participants should be aware that they are now changing from an open, information-gathering approach to a perspective focused on (potential) users. What perspective do they want to have? Looking at the simple process of preparing toast, this warm-up shows the different ways people approach a task (starting point of the preparation process; flavors; kitchen appliances, such as a pan, toaster, oven; organization of the purchase).
In addition to technical preferences, personal needs will be recognized – like creating a cozy ambiance, taking care of family members, or eating in peace.

8–10 min

Material:
Sheets of paper and pens ● The "Draw Toast" exercise was written by Dave Gray, one of the authors of Gamestorming, https://gamestorming.com/draw-toast/

BACK STORIES

Participants group themselves into pairs. Have each pair sit back-to-back in the room.

1 In five minutes, person A tells person B about their most exciting experience in the last six months. Person B listens.

2 Person B now has two minutes to describe how they perceived person A. Encourage interpretations, such as, "I noticed that you were particularly relieved when it was all over." Or "You said you didn't go out at night. I guess it was because it was too dangerous for you."

3 The partners now switch roles and person B tells person A about their most exciting experience in five minutes.

4 Person A shares their perceptions of person B's story for two minutes.

Reflection
The warm-up is designed to encourage participants to listen carefully and then draw conclusions from what they have heard. What did you notice in particular? When did you realize something that your partner may not have noticed themselves yet? The back-to-back situation sharpens auditory and tactile senses. Because participants are only listening, it is easier to notice details. The interpretation step allows participants to practice verbalizing the impressions they have gathered. The step of looking for "what's behind what's heard" is essential for the "Synthesize" phase in Design Thinking.

 approx. 15 min

 Sample questions:
Most exciting experience? • Last important acquisition? • Best vacation? Craziest hobby? • Most strenuous handicraft experience?

SYNTHESIZE

In the "Synthesize" phase, the challenge is formulated in a new and more precise way with a focus on the user. To do this, first you must identify their really important, unmet needs. The next step is to develop user-centric solutions.

You have about 20 minutes to share, structure, and interpret the most interesting and inspiring interview findings. Determine the most important information gathered during the observation phase. Then, decide which user you want to continue working with (about ten minutes). Work out the persona (about 15 minutes) and record the need as defined from their point of view (about ten minutes).

1 Share your interview findings
- ○ Evaluate which findings from the interviews are most interesting.
- ○ Summarize and interpret the information: tensions, contradictions, feelings, moods, striking gestures, and facial expressions.
- ○ Gain clarity regarding assumptions and hypotheses.

2 Structure and determine relevant topics
- ○ Arrange all findings and put them into (new) groups.
- ○ Name the new groupings.
- ○ Highlight the most important findings.

3 Define the point of view
- ○ Select a need and user to continue working with.
- ○ Describe the user (persona).
- ○ What is the need of this user?

REFLECTION ...

Kolko, J. (2011): *Exposing the Magic of Design: A Practitioner's Guide to the Methods and Theory of Synthesis,* Oxford University Press.

SYNTHESIZE STEP-BY-STEP

> ## "SYNTHESIS IS AN ABDUCTIVE SENSEMAKING PROCESS. THROUGH EFFORTS OF DATA MANIPULATION, ORGANIZATION, PRUNING, AND FILTERING, DESIGNERS PRODUCE INFORMATION AND KNOWLEDGE."
>
> JON KOLKO

In the "Synthesize" phase, a so-called **"reframing"** of the original challenge takes place. The "Understand" and "Observe" phases help to shed more light on the topic and to find out what needs and problems potential users have in relation to the topic. It is important to consider many options and points of view.

In contrast, the "Synthesize" phase focuses the challenge, so it is seen only from the user's point of view. The challenge is redefined based on information gathered from users during field research.

A. STORYTELLING
This phase begins with storytelling. The team members tell each other what they have experienced or observed in the field interviews. Storytelling can be structured using various methods and tools. Examples are a) a table with the headings **interviewee – quotes/observations – findings – overarching topics**, or b) an **Empathy Map** (see p. 57).

 Kolko, J. (2010): Abductive thinking and sensemaking: The drivers of design synthesis. *Design Issues*, 26(1), p. 17.

B. WHAT'S HIDDEN BEHIND THE ANSWERS?

After the storytelling part, the point is to interpret what has been said or observed. The team asks, "What could be hidden behind the answers?" In this step of the analysis, the team adds another level to the statement or observation and tries to identify the motives and needs of the interviewees or the people they observed.

It also helps to cluster statements and to collect topics that are found in various interviews. The step from "what is said" to "what is known" is not easy because the team takes a step forward and adds an interpretation level to the user's statement. Don't worry if your interpretations are wrong. If this happens, you will find out new information during the testing of prototypes. Then, new ideas can be generated and tested with another iteration. Do not combine or change user statements at this point. It is important to interpret original statements when designing for users.

C. POINT OF VIEW DEFINITION

Once the team has interpreted all the exciting, contradictory, and interesting statements, the next step is to make a decision regarding which user knowledge should be used in further work. Different decision-making tools, like nuggeting (each team member sticks a Post-it to the statement he/she finds most interesting and writes why this statement is particularly exciting), can be utilized. A two-axis chart can also be used. Here, interesting statements are arranged along a vertical and horizontal axis, which can be labeled arbitrarily (e.g. extreme users versus many users, physical needs versus emotional needs, etc.). The team can move through several voting and decision phases.

After a user statement or piece of knowledge has been selected, it is recorded in a point of view description: user + statement + need. Alternatively, only user + need can be used here. The initial phrases "We have met …" (user), "We were surprised to learn/observe …" (statement/observation), "We want to help them (to feel like) …" (need) are helpful.

The point of view description serves as a starting point for a more precise, redefined Design Challenge based on the user's perspective.

HOW MIGHT WE ... TEMPLATE

HOW CAN WE HELP .... ,

....

TO ....

AND THEREBY ....

....

....

Example
"How can we help Thomas as a frequent traveler (44 years, father of two children, living in a small village with 5,000 inhabitants, who enjoys going out into nature in his spare time, jogging a lot and riding a racing bike, and often has to commute to foreign cities for work) to orientate himself better in cities so he can arrive relaxed at his destination?"

D. PERSON-AHA

It is important to have a detailed and unified view of the person behind the point of view description, the person who offered an "AHA" moment. For this, collages, sketches, photos from the interview, and/or context descriptions can be useful. This helps keep team members from falling back into their own assumptions and perspectives of the problem. These images can also be used to remind the team again and again of the person they are creating solutions for in the following phases.

At this point, we give two persona templates to the workshop participants to fill out to help teams agree on and describe a common persona. In the beginning, many teams find it difficult to commit to this persona, because they are afraid their decision will result in mistakes later. Don't overthink this – it is better to compromise than to fight. The persona will continue to be developed and changed as you gather more information in the following stages.

a) Persona Template

Most importantly, this template shows a unified vision for the team. It is important to understand the person's stage in life, what they like to do, what their life plans are, and their strengths and weaknesses. It is also helpful to give the person a face. Adapt the questions in our template to your context as needed.

As the process continues, you can alter and add to the persona again and again or even scrap it completely and work with a new persona.

b) Empathy Map

The Empathy Map helps the team to get to know the person in greater detail to empathize more deeply with their way of thinking.

We recommend that you proceed as follows:

1 Say and Do
Write down together what is obvious, that is, what you can hear or see. Put yourself back in the interview situation again. What did you ask the interviewees and how did they respond? Make compromises and move forward. Do not get stuck on details. As always, this can be changed and adapted later. The main purpose of this discussion is to reach an initial agreement within the group.

2 Think and Feel
Once you have collected the obvious points, turn to assumptions: what does the persona think? What does she not tell you or others? What concerns or questions does she keep to herself? Often these things have to do with the current life situation or plans that have not yet been realized (next big life event). Finally, turn to the "Feel" area. This is the most important area, because needs arise in the context of feelings. Try to stay balanced between positive and negative feelings. At this point, it helps some teams to ask themselves the question of what drives the persona in principle or how they feel about the concrete situation.

Gumienny, R., Lindberg, T., & Meinel, C. (2011): Exploring the synthesis of information in design processes – opening the black-box.

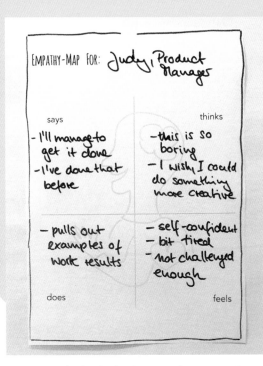

Examples for the development of a Person-AHA

Depending on the challenge, additional tools can also be used to record user statements and observations.

"CUSTOMERS DON'T JUST BUY PRODUCTS, THEY HIRE THEM TO DO A JOB."

CLAYTON CHRISTENSEN

Jobs-to-be-done (short: JTBD)

The jobs-to-be-done approach is particularly suitable for recording user statements and observations in their specific context. Or have users fill in the tool themselves or let them think aloud.

Ted Levitt laid the foundation for the JTBD method with a now well-known statement: "Customers don't want a drill, but a hole in the wall." (Ted Levitt, 1960). Thus, it is not a question of a specific product or an exact product class, but the needs that the user wishes to have fulfilled.

Based on Levitt's finding, Harvard business school professor Clayton Christensen introduced the term "job." Accordingly, a job is the task that a product or service fulfills for its users. This job is why someone uses or buys the product or service. The special thing about the JTBD method is that there is a change of perspective away from the product and toward its benefits. It opens the solution space. Ideas outside the existing product category suddenly come into view.

The tool also becomes easy to understand with the well-known example of a large American fast food chain (see reference on p. 61). Their goal was to increase the sale of their milkshakes. A team of design researchers conducted many observations and qualitative interviews to understand exactly what purpose the product serves. The company could then consider how they wanted to change or expand the product.

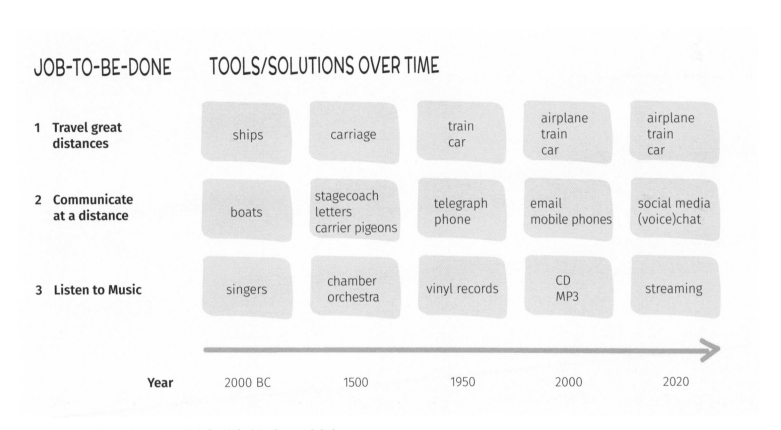

JOB-TO-BE-DONE   TOOLS/SOLUTIONS OVER TIME

Job-to-be-done	2000 BC	1500	1950	2000	2020
1 Travel great distances	ships	carriage	train car	airplane train car	airplane train car
2 Communicate at a distance	boats	stagecoach letters carrier pigeons	telegraph phone	email mobile phones	social media (voice)chat
3 Listen to Music	singers	chamber orchestra	vinyl records	CD MP3	streaming
Year	2000 BC	1500	1950	2000	2020

JTBD Examples to Distinguish Between "Jobs" and Final Products or Solutions

Taken from **Šáchová-Kleisli, A., & Walther, B. (2015):** Job-to-be-done-Logik in der Praxis. *Marketing Review St. Gallen*, 32(1), p. 3. (GER)

JOBS-TO-BE-DONE TEMPLATE

USER ....

(short description of person, activity, experience, and/or important characteristics)

SITUATION

(Give a short description of the situation in which the problem or need occurs.)

WHEN ....

MOTIVATION

(What is the user's need or motivation in this situation?)

THEN THEY WOULD LIKE TO ....

DESIRED RESULT

(Choose a formulation and describe what should be achieved. What is the ultimate goal?)

THEN THEY WOULD LIKE TO ....

SO THAT THEY CAN ....

IN ORDER TO ACHIEVE ....

EXAMPLE INTERCOM:

When an important new customer signs up,

I want to be notified

so I can start a conversation with them.

With the JTBD tool, you describe the problem or the need you've discovered. Who is/are the user(s)? In which situation does the need arise? How can the need or the motivation of the user be described in detail? What would you like to achieve with your solution?

If a user description does not exist yet, you can add this to the template.

Clayton Christensen explains JTBD using the milkshake example: https://www.youtube.com/watch?time_continue=77&v=sfGtw2C95Ms

"You can't use up creativity.
The more you use,
the more you have."

Maya Angelou

04

IDEATE

5 WAYS TO USE

The participants form three or four teams.

- Each team gets an item, for example, a mug, a credit card, a paper clip, or a cable. (You can choose anything.) Each team member receives a sheet of paper and a pen.
- In five minutes, each participant comes up with as many alternative uses as possible for the team's object (at least five!) and draws them (or briefly describes them).
- The idea is to develop uses for the object. Each team member now has two minutes to share their ideas with the others on the team.

Reflection

The warm-up serves to loosen up and allow unusual and wild ideas. "Out-of-the-box thinking" is stimulated. Many ideas should emerge in a short time, without reconsidering or directly evaluating them.

 11–13 min

 Material:
Sheets of paper and pens, any objects, for example, cup, debit card, paper clip, cable, stone, chalk ...

I'M A TREE

All participants stand in a circle.

- The moderator steps into the middle of the circle and begins to tell a story. For example: "I am a tree and my branches move in the wind." The person also acts out their narrative with facial expressions, gestures, movement such as wiggling the arms and moving the upper body from left to right.
- A second person joins the first person in the circle and adds to the scene. For example: "I am a red apple hanging from this branch."
- A third person joins in and adds to the story scene. When the third participant has joined, the original presenter leaves position and rejoins the circle. A fourth person steps in and adds to the story ...
- This goes on and on ... The person who has been in the scene for the longest time always steps out and rejoins the circle.

Reflection

The warm-up serves to playfully build positive team spirit and helps the group find a creative flow. The storytelling from person to person embodies the mindset, "building on the ideas of others" and thus seamlessly leads into the "Ideate" phase.

5–10 min

Mindset:
Building on what has been said and further developing other people's stories.

IDEATE

 In the "Ideate" phase it is important to develop as many ideas as possible – based on the point of view you have selected. Different brainstorming techniques help to illuminate different dimensions of the need.

 You have about 45 minutes to create a "How might we …?" brainstorming question, based on the point of view selected, and to try out different brainstorming techniques. At the end of this phase, the team should select one or two ideas to continue working with.

 1 Brainstorming Session
- ○ Formulate a "How might we …?" question.
- ○ Silent brainstorming – try to come up with at least 20 ideas in five minutes.
- ○ Object brainstorming (see p. 70)
- ○ Idea train (see p. 71)
- ○ Hot potato (see p. 70)
- ○ Bring an internal competition into the phase (e.g. each team presents the two best and two weakest solutions at halftime).

2 Selection of Ideas
- ○ Look at all the ideas again. Are there clusters of ideas?

Examples of Possible Clusters
- Fits the question – exciting – outside the reference frame
- Today – Tomorrow – Future Vision
- What idea would the user love?
- Which idea is the most radical?
- Which idea is the easiest to implement?
- Choose one or two ideas within the team for the next phase.

REFLECTION ...

Curedale, R. (2013): *50 Brainstorming Methods: For team and individual ideation,* Design Community College. **Von Schmieden, Taheri & Mayer, online course:** https://open.hpi.de/courses/ideas2018

- Formulate the "How might we ...?" question or "jobs-to-be-done."
- Explain the rules for brainstorming.
- Draw the Idea Selection Matrix on paper or whiteboard.

1 Plan time (e.g. 45 minutes for brainstorming, divided into three different brainstorming methods).

2 Silent brainstorming – everyone collects their first ideas and writes them down on Post-its. The ideas should be based on the "How might we ...?" question or "jobs-to-be-done" formulation.

3 Everyone reads their ideas aloud and puts them into the matrix. It is important not to evaluate the ideas immediately. Don't discuss them!

4 Now we can discuss. How would your persona rate the ideas? What ideas would she like best? How can the "HOW" ideas be realized?

5 Which ideas should be developed further with prototypes?

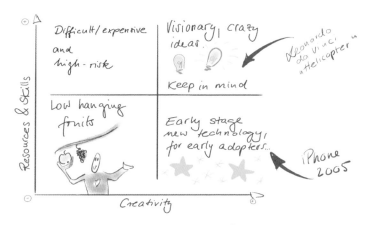

IDEA SELECTION MATRIX

Explanation of the How-Now-Wow Matrix by Dave Gray:
https://gamestorming.com/how-now-wow-matrix/

68

IDEATE METHODS

Brainstorming Methods

- Throw out many different kinds of ideas (for example, in a classic initial brainstorming interaction, where every idea is recorded on a Post-it).
- Look at something from a different perspective (e.g. the participants put themselves in a different time).
- Access other types of ideas through physical movement or changing the position of their bodies.

We recommend using three to five different methods in a team and increasing the creativity with every iteration. It is a good idea to start each brainstorming session with a specific question, for example:

- Which functionalities are absolutely necessary for the user?
- How would we tackle this challenge in 2050?

Idea generation using the starfish method on the topic of mobility needs of Millenials in the Design Thinking Laboratory of the University of Biberach

6-3-5 Method: Sheets of paper are divided into 18 boxes with three columns and six rows and distributed to each of the six participants in the team. Each participant formulates three ideas in the first line for a given question (one idea per column). After three to five minutes, everyone passes the sheet clockwise at the same time and the ideas are further developed.

Building on the Ideas of Others: Each participant selects an idea created by someone else, and develops three further ideas that build on it. Share these with the group as idea clusters on the whiteboard.

2050: The participants jump mentally into the year 2050 to develop wilder and future-oriented ideas. Here everything is possible and technical feasibility is not limited. Use one Post-it per idea.

Object Brainstorming: The observation of an object (arbitrarily chosen) invites participants to question what the object could be used for and thus represents a new source of inspiration for free association.

Negative Brainstorming: This aims at collecting ideas that would not solve the problem, but rather would make the situation worse. This perspective makes it possible to analyze the weak points of a problem. The negative ideas can then be transformed back into helpful ideas with the help of reverse brainstorming.

Hot Potato: Participants throw around an object – the hot potato. The person catching the hot potato should say an idea for a solution. Since the potato is "hot," this should happen at a fast pace.

Starfish: If the brainstorming of the team members takes place lying down, in the form of a starfish (see photo on p. 69), the change of the spatial and physical perspective supports the flow of new thoughts for the ideation. The team members spontaneously say aloud their thoughts for a solution and inspire each other. A person can sit in the middle of the starfish and record the ideas (one idea per Post-it).

IDEATE METHODS 02

Photo Brainstorming: Use different magazines (e.g. from the fields of lifestyle, architecture, or innovation) to select a photo that you find inspiring in the context of the Design Challenge (individually). In a limited time of about five minutes, write down keywords for the photo you have chosen. It is important to record everything that comes to mind without evaluating the ideas. This makes free association possible.

Idea Train: Armed with Post-its and pencils, the train leaves! As you walk in a line, say the ideas out loud and write them down, then stick them on the back of the person in front of you. Use one idea per Post-it, so you can sort them later on the whiteboard.

Brainwriting: Each participant writes three ideas for the Design Challenge on a separate piece of paper. Pass these idea sheets to neighboring team members in several rounds, supplementing or developing them further. At the end of a brainwriting process, numerous ideas can be discussed and prioritized in the group.

Semantic Intuition: Randomly connect concepts with each other in order to gain new ideas from them. On Post-its, write down all the terms that come to mind about the topic. Mix the pieces of paper in a box, then pull out two pieces of paper and connect these two thoughts with each other ...

The 5 Whys: Ask why five times, then you'll know the true cause of the problem! Formulate the problem in writing. Now comes the first why: Why is the problem the way it is? Write an answer to the first why question. The answer becomes the second why question: Why is that so? And so on ...

 Brainstorming posters: https://bit.ly/2Wj3ZOc (GER)

IDEA PROFILE TEMPLATE

**Sketch your idea here
(Visualization)**

**Describe your idea here
PURPOSE**

**What do you do to realize the purpose?
RESULT**

**How do you design the implementation?
PROCESS**

Photo Brainstorming

"Everyone has ideas. They may be too busy or lack the confidence or technical ability to carry them out. But I want to carry them out. It is a matter of getting up and doing it."

James Dyson

05

PROTOTYPE

WARM-UP
PAPER PLANES

The participants form teams of 2 or 3. Each team gets a sheet of paper.

- Together, in silence, each team builds a paper airplane in two minutes that flies as far as possible. An additional challenge is that each participant uses their nondominant hand (i.e. right-handers build with their left hand).
- After two minutes, each team writes the names of the team members on the plane.
- All teams bring their planes to a starting line and throw their planes at the same time.
  (Variation: Throw with the weak arm.)
- Everyone cheers for the winning team – the one whose paper airplane flew the farthest.

Reflection
The warm-up serves to get into action mode and "think with your hands." The aim of the "Prototype" phase is to quickly and easily make the idea physically tangible (for products) or perceptible (for services). Focus on building together and not on discussing how each individual would build it themselves.

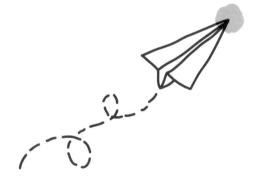

 5 min

 Material:
Sheets of paper

WARM-UP
10 THINGS IN A PAPER BAG

Each participant brings a paper bag, which they have filled with contents. On the day of the workshop, there are several ways to use the bags and their contents.

1 Guess who brought which bag with them
The participants are asked not to show their bags to anyone beforehand and to simply hand them in on arrival. Then each participant takes a bag (not their own) and tries to guess who filled the bag. If the person does not guess after one minute, the owner of the bag reveals himself or herself.

2 Silent Prototyping
Form teams of four to five people. Each participant lays out the contents of their bag for everyone on their team to see.

The teams are asked to build a prototype using the items they brought with them.

Examples of Tasks:
- Fast prototype for the workshop topic
- Prototype for the optimal creative space
- Prototype for good team communication

To keep it from being too easy, ask the teams not to talk during prototyping; they should just try to build on the ideas of others. The teams then explain to each other how the prototypes work and what everyone was thinking.

Reflection
It is exciting to see how differently the task is interpreted and which objects are created. Participants learn some exciting details from others that open up new perspectives. In silent prototyping, the prohibition on talking prevents teams from being "overly sophisticated." Instead, they just start building, which is important in the "Prototype" phase. When presenting the prototypes, the participants are usually surprised by the ideas that arise and how these encourage creativity.

Guessing: per participant approx. 1 min.
Silent Prototyping: 10 min + approx. 3 min
Presentation: 3 min per team

Material: paper bags
Preparation: Participants are asked to put ten different (nonvaluable) things in the bag beforehand and bring it to the workshop. The participants should not receive any further tips about why they are doing this or what the bags are needed for.

PHASE
PROTOTYPE

 The "Prototype" phase is about bringing an idea into a form so that potential users can evaluate it. For this purpose, tangible prototypes are built, so users have something to interact with. As time goes by, the prototypes become more complex.

 You have about 45 minutes to convert the idea into one or more prototypes. Visualizations, models, Lego landscapes, or role plays are all options to bring the idea to life. Before you begin, think about how testers (users) will experience and evaluate the prototypes in the next phase.

 1 Sketches and Realizations
- What is the main function of the prototype?
- What needs should the prototype fulfill (from the user's point of view)?
- What components should the prototype consist of?
- Start with paper and pen prototypes to sketch out the main function.
- What exactly does the prototype look like?
- How does the prototype feel?
- How does the prototype work and how does it behave exactly?
- Be good enough: Adapt the prototype to the respective project phase so that it is just good enough.
- Be fast: Try to build quickly in the initial phases of a project!

REFLECTION ...

 Adenauer, J. & Petruschat, J. (2012): *Prototype! physical, virtual, hybrid, smart: tackling new challenges in design and engineering* ● **HPI-Stanford Design Thinking Research Program (2013):** Design Thinking Prototyping Cardset. ● **Mayer, von Schmieden & Taheri, online course:** https://open.hpi.de/courses/prototype2019

A few suggestions for expectations regarding the development of prototypes:

Design Thinking is a user-centric approach, so feedback from users is gathered early in the process. Due to the haptic experience of a prototype, customers get a better idea of whether a product or service makes sense from the user's perspective. Neuroscience points out that the haptic experience of the unknown (e.g. a new product) enables a maximum level of perception and greatly increases the quality of any user statements (cf. Liedtka 2018, p. 77). The development of prototypes in Design Thinking is less about fine-tuning products or services and more about gaining information in iterative cycles with users. At the beginning of a new untested idea, it is useful to create simple, low-resolution prototypes that are often less precise than a minimally viable product from the start-up scene. Such prototypes can be created quickly and inexpensively to allow for flexibility for further development after testing.

Due to the character of unfinished things, prototypes invite users to participate in the development process and they enable a fast and resource-efficient failure.

The prototype is therefore not the sole result of the Design Thinking Process. Other results are:

- Insights that were gained together
- Sharpened perception of all participants
- Newly acquired and shared knowledge
- Better understanding of the customer
- Better products and services in the long-term

The creative process is triggered by group work in the first session. The actual results will only emerge with further work on the project, based on the original findings, by individual participants or in team meetings using methods from Design Thinking.

EXAMPLES OF PROTOTYPES

A role play as a prototype for the development of a new travel concept for students, Design Thinking Lab, University of Biberach

Prototype city hall model for the visualization of different variants in the BIM Lab of the University of Biberach | Photo: Stefan Sättele

Prototyping with Lego on the topic of the intensification of interdepartmental cooperation

A storyboard as a prototype for a sales training course for bank consultants that deviates from the traditional consulting model

SOME PROTOTYPE METHODS IN DETAIL 01

Prototype Method	Material	Degree of Detail*			Suitable for ...
		low	medium	high	
Sketch	Paper or digital, sketched or scribbled, on a flip-chart or sheets of paper or Post-its.	✓			As the first step from idea to prototype, everything, products + services (storyboards)
Mock-up	Shows the overall impression of a system without needing to be functional.		✓		Digital + physical products
Wireframe	Early conceptual design of a system. Shows functional aspects and the ideal arrangement of elements.	✓			Website
Diagram	Shows the order. Linked ideas can be tested, shown how the experience changes over time.	✓	✓		Website
Paper	Construction or enrichment of objects and products with paper or cardboard.	✓			Digital + physical products, miniatures, architecture, accessories
Storytelling and story writing	Communicating or presenting sequences and stories.	✓	✓	✓	Experiences, service prototypes
Storyboards	The end-to-end customer journey shown through a series of pictures or sketches.	✓	✓		Experiences, service prototypes
Business model	Systematic representation of business relationships, and systems, for example, with a business model canvas or lean canvas.	✓	✓	✓	Business models
Bodystorming	Reproduction of specific situations through physical activities performed by the project team members.	✓			Physical experiences

SOME PROTOTYPE METHODS IN DETAIL 02

Prototype Method	Material	Degree of Detail*			Suitable for ...
		low	medium	high	
Video	Recording and presentation of even complex scenarios.	✓	✓		Experiences, services, marketing ideas
Photo	Photomontage for the simulated representation of a situation. Additional image processing software can be used if needed.	✓			Products, digital and physical experiences
Physical model	Two-dimensional idea embodied in three dimensions. Can be created with 3D printing, but also by building with other materials, such as Lego.	✓			Rooms, processes, structures
Role play	Service and experience prototypes can be easily integrated into role-plays. Props, costumes, and precise dialogue help to present the desired situation with as much detail as possible. Thus, testers can really experience the situation and do not need to work hard to imagine the idea, as they would if it were hypothetical (e.g. with only a description).	✓	✓		Experiences, service prototypes
Minimum viable product (MVP)	Executable version of a system or a version, with only the most essential function.	✓	✓	✓	Digital products, software
Service blueprinting	Structured description of services for the comprehensive experience design of an end-to-end customer journey.	✓	✓	✓	Products, digital and physical services

* low: in early phase, medium: initial solutions, high: more final solutions

Tables taken and supplemented by Lewrick, et al. (2017):
The Design Thinking Playbook. München: Vahlen. (GER)

"In the real world, the smartest people are people who make mistakes and learn. In school, the smartest people don't make mistakes."

Robert Kiyosaki

06

TEST

1-2-3 HOORAY!

Each participant finds a partner.

Round 1
Take turns counting to three and keep repeating while getting faster and faster, like this:
Person A: "one," Person B: "two," Person A: "three,"
Person B: "one," Person A: "two" …

Round 2
Replace the two with one clap, like this:
Person A: "one," Person B: "claps hands together,"
Person A: "three." Person B: "one," Person A: "claps hands together" …

Round 3
Now change the three by snapping your fingers, like this:
Person A: "one," Person B: "clap," Person A: "snap,"
Person B: "one," Person A: "clap," Person B: "snap" …

Round 4
Every time someone makes a mistake or the wrong gesture, the other partners raise their hands in the air and scream "Hooray," cheering the mistake together.

Reflection
The warm-up serves to emphasize the principle of "fail early and often" and to understand it as a normal part of the learning process in projects. Fast trial and error, construction, and testing enables cost- and resource-efficient progress while finding new solutions. Prototypes are not ready-made solutions, but provide new insights for improvements. If the idea is not liked by the user, the team goes into iteration loops.

 10 min

 Short:
Round 1: 1-2-3
Round 2: 1-clap-3
Round 3: 1-clap-snap
Round 4: 1-clap-snap-HOORAY!

WARM-UP
FREE FALL

The participants form three or four teams (depending on the number of participants).

- Every team gets a box full of specific items (see below).
- The teams have ten minutes to build an object that is later dropped from a certain height (at least from the first floor of a building). All materials must be used in the object. The goal is to create an object that falls as slowly as possible.
- After ten minutes, all teams drop their prototypes, one after another, from the same height, while recording the time. The winner is the team with the longest fall time.

Reflection
The warm-up serves to get people thinking about the testing scenario during the development of an idea. Some teams get stuck in a discussion about how to build something, while others may focus on trying to use all the materials. However, others quickly enter into their own test phase, where they build and test their object iteratively.

15 min

Materials:*
One box per team: feathers, five Lego bricks, one glue stick, ten cotton pads, three meters of string, five rubber bands, ten sheets of paper, five long wooden skewers

*It is important that all teams are equipped with exactly the same materials.

PHASE
TEST

 The "Test" phase is about testing the prototype(s) with users. The prototype represents only the current knowledge and assumptions the team has about the user.

 You have 20 minutes to prepare the test scenario and test it with a customer or feedback provider who is not a member of your team. Go into the testing situation with open eyes and ears. See if you have recognized the need correctly. Collect user feedback and stay open to new insights.

Here it can be helpful to use ad hoc documentation to convey the common thread that ultimately led to the solution approaches and prototypes. Therefore, in workshops, we like to plan an intermediate step, "Documentation," before testing. As part of this task, the teams compile the results of the individual steps in a compressed form on two flipchart sheets or a sheet of brown paper. This will give you a good overview of your "journey" through the session.

 1 Prepare Test Scenario
- ○ What does your test scenario look like?
- ○ Formulate open questions for the test scenario.
- ○ Where can we find interested testers?
- ○ Define role distribution. (Who speaks? Who takes notes?)

2 Perform Testing
- ○ Explain the reason for testing. Build trust.
- ○ Do not conduct sales negotiations.
- ○ Ask open questions.
- ○ Let the subject think aloud, don't interrupt.
- ○ Comply with the 20:80 rule.
- ○ Allow for silence.
- ○ Ask for moods, feelings.
- ○ Show gratitude.

3 Collect Feedback
- ○ What worked/what did the user like? Why?
- ○ What didn't work/what didn't the user like? Why?
- ○ Were there any ambiguities? Did the tester have any questions?
- ○ New ideas, suggestions.
- ○ In the end, you can also ask in which settings and situations the prototype would be useful.

REFLECTION ...

 Mayer, von Schmieden & Taheri, online course: https://open.
hpi.de/courses/prototype2019 ● **HPI-Stanford Design Thinking
Research Program (2013):** Design Thinking Prototyping Cardset.
● **Online course "Basics of Design Testing":** https://open.sap.
com/courses/ut1-2

TEST

Feedback grid
To collect user feedback for future iteration steps

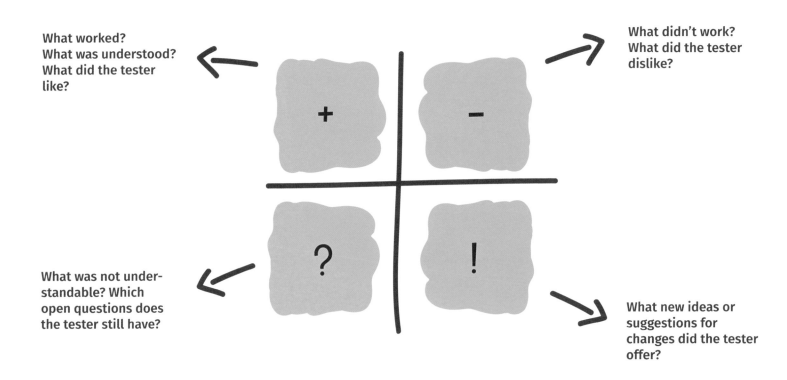

What worked?
What was understood?
What did the tester
like?

What didn't work?
What did the tester
dislike?

What was not under-
standable? Which
open questions does
the tester still have?

What new ideas or
suggestions for
changes did the tester
offer?

A tester interacts with a prototype in the Design Thinking Laboratory of the University of Biberach

Example of feedback collected during the test phase

DOCUMENTATION
ITERATION
IV

DOCUMENTATION

Experiences gained from our workshops show again and again how important it is for teams to document the core aspects of each step, as soon as possible.

On the one hand, the common thread that flows through the different steps is brought into view again.

On the other hand, we often find that teams see the developed prototypes as the result of the collaborative session. However, this type of focused, collaborative work is more likely to be found in the preparatory phase of a project. As we have already explained, real creativity emerges slowly and unconsciously, without pressure. This typically takes place outside concentrated work phases.

This documentation step ensures that the valuable information and ideas that inspired the ideation and development of the first prototypes are saved.

Document the phases and their intermediate results in order to internally communicate the results later and to use this information to develop the project further. It is thus important to take photos of the results of the teamwork (walls, boards, flip-charts, Post-it collages ...) from time to time throughout the day.

In addition, the ad hoc documentation prevents participants from accepting ideas and prototypes as the day's results, but instead helps them be aware of and understand the value of each individual phase.

You can summarize the individual results in a compressed form on two flipchart sheets or on a sheet of brown paper. Following are some examples.

Flipchart Sheet 1:

UNDERSTAND – Use the Post-its on which you have noted the cluster names or main questions from this phase (e.g. general conditions, goal, budget, concerns, target group ...).

OBSERVE – List the different research tools you have used and give a quantitative impression (e.g. five interviews, three internet articles, two expert lectures, two book excerpts, three self-experiments ...).

SYNTHESIZE – Take advantage of the Post-its and templates you have created during this step. Give a keyword-like overview of the main findings you have gained from the observation results. What topics have you selected to use for your persona? What insights have you formulated?

Attach your completed persona templates to the documentation sheet.

Explain how you developed your question for the "Ideation" phase. (How might we question?)

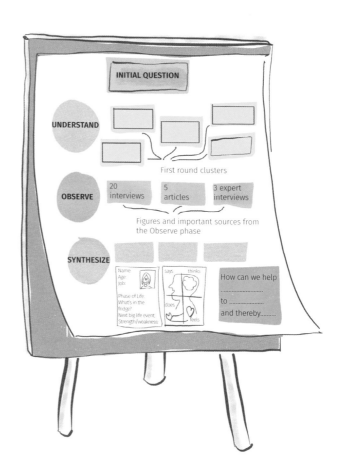

Flipchart Sheet 2:

IDEATE – Select only those ideas you later used for prototyping.

PROTOTYPE – Later you can insert photos of your prototype(s). For the final presentation, you can use the original prototype, of course.

TEST – Print out the feedback grid that we presented on p. 90 or draw it on the flipchart here. In the TEST phase, you will then note the feedback that the testers have given you.

In the final step, the results are presented in the form of a pitch. We recommend the following timeframe:

- Preparation of the documentation in advance on the basis of the intermediate results (5 minutes).
- Presentation of Flipchart Sheet 1 (3–5 minutes).
- Presentation of Flipchart Sheet 2 and prototypes (5 minutes).
- Get feedback on the presentation and take notes (5 minutes).

A comprehensive, organized documentation is the basis for further iterations and future collaborative work on the project.

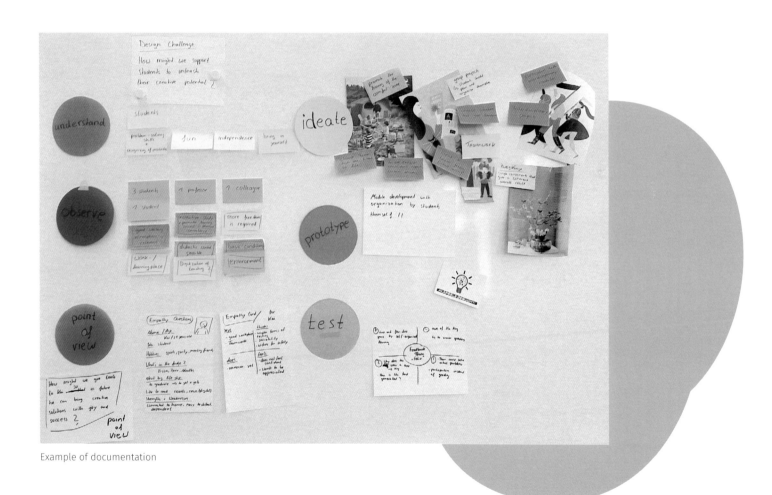

Example of documentation

ITERATION

The principle of iteration is an essential element in Design Thinking. This is when the team looks back at one or more steps and examines what it has done so far from a different perspective. Early exchange with (potential) users and/or experts is essential. We therefore recommend that you record feedback after every round in a structured way within the team:

- What you've learned
- What you're working on now
- Which phase you're reentering

Again and again, we meet workshop participants who hope that a single run of the Design Thinking cycle in a one- or two-day workshop will be sufficient to achieve a breakthrough by asking the right question or generating ideas. This might happen, but it is rather the exception. This isn't how Design Thinking is supposed to work.

In particular, people who have little experience with Design Thinking or who are involved in a Design Thinking activity for the first time often have a hard time going through the process. They often say about the last step: "If I had known we would keep using results from previous steps in every subsequent step, I would have approached the previous step differently."

These people may be disappointed because they blame themselves, the other team members, or the moderator for what they consider to be unsatisfactory results. This disappointment is understandable, especially when one considers that in the operative business often little more than a single day is planned for Design Thinking, with high expectations for implementable results.

Consider it this way: A single initial Design Thinking workshop serves as a basis for starting a longer project phase, which is structured with the help of Design Thinking. This first day, viewed in terms of the entire Design Thinking cycle, falls within the "Understand" phase. With the help of this first session, you will go through all the typical project phases but in a condensed form. This gives you the chance to identify possible obstacles in advance and to go back to the exact steps you would have liked to see. These steps can then also be performed by individuals or smaller teams over and over through various decision-making rounds.

One of our training participants put it this way: "Design Thinking is a desirable permanent state in which you constantly oscillate between the different steps, making assumptions that are then either verified or proven false.

Depending on this, you can either go further or jump back."

The individual Design Thinking phases are designed to help participants change the way they approach tasks within the team. It is difficult to change habits. Clear guidelines can help.

"ANY TIME YOU'RE TRYING TO CHANGE PEOPLE'S BEHAVIOR, YOU NEED TO START THEM OFF WITH A LOT OF STRUCTURE, SO THEY DON'T HAVE TO THINK. A LOT OF WHAT WE DO IS HABIT, AND IT'S HARD TO CHANGE THOSE HABITS, BUT HAVING VERY CLEAR GUARDRAILS CAN HELP US."

KAAREN HANSON

 Liedtka, J. (2018): Why Design Thinking Works. *Harvard Business Review*, September issue: 72–79. ● https://hbr.org/2018/09/why-design-thinking-works

WHY DO WARM-UPS? FURTHER LINKS

What Are Warm-ups For?
When working with Design Thinking, warm-ups help participants switch to an open and creative mode (see also Chapter II on Creativity). We mainly use three types of warm-ups.

1 Energizing Warm-ups
These warm-ups are used to get teams moving and using the whole body to activate the mind. Especially after lunch breaks or in the afternoon after a long work phase, this warm-up category is suitable to fill the room with energy and bring some momentum into the teams (e.g.: Danish Clapping, Ninja, Rock-Paper-Scissors).

2 Warm-ups Before the Individual Phases
Warm-ups at the beginning of a Design Thinking phase are designed to help teams prepare for the following work mode. For example, a warm-up can prepare for convergent or divergent thinking or focus on building empathy, listening carefully, or letting thoughts and ideas run wild. We have proposed at least one warm-up per phase in this book to facilitate the right attitude. Of course, there are more available.

Warm-up enthusiasts can browse the sources listed here for some more suitable examples.

3 Warm-ups for Team Development
Another variant of warm-ups is suitable for groups and teams that do not know each other well or when working together across different functions, disciplines, or companies. Short warm-ups quickly break the ice and bring teams together.

This category of warm-ups is particularly suitable at the beginning of joint project work or at the beginning of workshops with participants who do not know each other well (examples: 2 truths & 1 lie, semantic card, acquaintance bingo).

 D-school Stanford, The K12 Lab Wiki: https://dschool-old.stanford.edu/groups/k12/wiki/3091c/Improv_activities_for_Design_Thinking.html ● **HPI Warm-up Set, download:** https://hpi-academy.de/fileadmin/hpi-academy/Infobrosch%C3%B-Cren/WarmUp-Set_deutsch_-_HPI_Academy.pdf (GER) ● **Improv Encyclopedia:** http://improvencyclopedia.org/categories//Warm-up.html

WARM-UP EXAMPLES

How to make toast

Draw Houses, Design Thinking Lab of the University of Biberach

Paper Planes, Design Thinking Lab of the
University of Biberach

Blind Portrait

V

TEAM

TEAM

An important part of Design Thinking is intensive teamwork. It is a good idea to create teams with people who are different from one another. This allows teams to have many different perspectives and expertise for a broader view of the Design Challenge and different team strengths. Cooperation on projects across company silos is important for successful Design Thinking results. From the very beginning, teams from different company departments (e.g. Marketing, Finance, HR) should work together on projects in order to include all important aspects and ways of thinking, right from the start. This is in contrast to working along a value chain (waterfall principle), where, for example, HR first creates a concept, the finance department then offsets the draft, and finally, marketing determines that the idea does not meet the needs of any target group at all.

Team research (input-process-output model) has shown that processes have more influence on the results of teams than other elements (such as team composition or formulation of the challenge or the design prompt). Process variables include, for example, how the team communicates, how it is led or managed ("leadership"), and psychological security. This last element was identified as the most important variable for successful teamwork in Google's large-scale team study (re:Work, 2012). As the name implies, "psychological security" refers to a feeling of security in a team; for example, one is not ostracized or punished by other team members (or the manager) if one freely expresses their thoughts and ideas (Edmondson, 1999). This is particularly important in a creative or innovation-driven work environment, which is characterized by uncertainty about both the solution and the problem itself.

In Design Thinking the conscious design of the work is part of the mindset, in order to achieve an open and creativity-enhancing atmosphere. The most common principles, which we also communicate in our workshops, are:

1 WORK AS VISUALLY AS POSSIBLE

2 BUILD ON THE IDEAS OF OTHERS

3 RESIST CRITICISM AND JUDGMENT

4 ALLOW WILD, UNUSUAL IDEAS

5 THINK USER-CENTERED

6 FULL ATTENTION FOR THE SPEAKER, NO PARALLEL CONVERSATIONS

TEAM HI + BYE

TEAM HI

Rituals play an important role in collaborative work (e.g. Ozenc & Hagan, 2018). For example, at the beginning of team or project work, it is important to take the time to arrive (Edmondson & Harvey, 2018). A good basis for uninhibited cooperation and a positive team atmosphere is created by taking the time to get to know one another. For example, the team members can talk about what is on their minds, where they come from, what they are working on both privately and professionally and/or their expectations for the day.

The coach or workshop leader should ensure that every team member participates, even if some will contribute more and some less. Post-its can help, especially in larger teams (one Post-it per person per category; see figure). The "Hi-Round" is particularly effective if it is conducted – after a detailed introductory session – briefly at the beginning of each collaborative working day. This creates a daily ritual for entering in the team and normalizes the regular sharing of each person's individual emotional status. In any case, a clear time-frame should be set for the Hi-Round.

Possible questions might include:

- How do you describe the core of your personal brand? What expectations do you have regarding the day/cooperation/team?
- What do you bring to the team? What is your team strength? What is your team weakness?
- How are you today? What do you want to share with the team? What is important for the upcoming cooperation?
- Which topic is currently of particular private/professional interest to you?
- Who was your superhero in your childhood?
- What was your career dream as a child?
- Which animal represents you best? Draw it and then explain the reference to your team members.

Example of a Team Hi-Round

TEAM BYE

At the end of the group work, a short "Bye-Round" is a good idea. The Team Bye should be anchored in the agenda as a fixed item of the day at the beginning; otherwise, it may be skipped due to a lack of time and low energy levels.

The "Bye" serves to give each team member the opportunity to share with the team, about the day itself, or their state of mind, to address both satisfaction or displeasure with the cooperation.

The following questions are suitable for this purpose, for example, or a more detailed round of "I like …, I wish …" depending on the needs of the team (see next section).

Possible Questions:

- What else is on your mind and what do you want to tell the others before leaving today?
- In one sentence per person, what do you think of the content of the work today? In one sentence, what did you think of the teamwork today?
- What went well in the team today? What would you wish for the next time, so the work could be better?
- What are you thinking about? Two sentences per team member.

TEAM FEEDBACK I LIKE ..., I WISH ...

As a method for team feedback, we like to use "I like, I wish." This can be useful both at the end of the cooperation and (several times) during longer collaborative projects.

The procedure is similar to a 360° feedback round. Everyone writes one Post-it for each team member:

I LIKE
What you liked about them, how they especially helped the team.

I WISH
What they could show more of in the future, what they could improve on for even better cooperation.

We also like to use this tool for a general workshop reflection (see the chapter on Sample Agendas). The coach or workshop leader thus receives feedback from all participants about the day. There we add a third category, "I will ... (do) in the future."

IMPORTANT TIPS

Feedback is a gift!
When someone else takes the time to hold a mirror up to you, that enables you to see your reflection. If you receive feedback, listen and thank them at that moment without going into a defensive, explanative or argumentative mode!

Write yourself feedback!
In order to bring the self-image and the external image together, everyone should also write down feedback for themselves. Self-obsessed people should also be self-critical and pessimists should also take time to praise themselves.

 **Source:** https://ilikeiwish.org/

Team Feedback

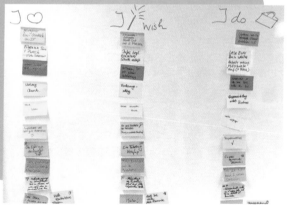

TEAM ROLES

Especially if a team has been working together for a longer period, distributing roles can support creative teamwork. If desired, they can also be redistributed at every meeting. We often assign these roles in our workshops:

- **Lead:** summarize statements, and
  - if the team goes too far off the mark, this person leads them back,
  - when the team gets unfocused, they call a break.
- **Space:** prepare the work area, clean up after the meetings and in between, so that there is a good, creative working atmosphere.
- **Documentation:** document and summarize the important contents and steps after the meeting.
- **Timekeeper:** make sure that the team stays within the estimated timeframe, remind team members how much time is still remaining for the step and reset the stopwatch for each step.
- **Motivator:** recognize when the energy in the team dwindles, motivate the team to try out new ideation methods during the ideate process, or suggest warm-ups to take a break from the teamwork for a short time and restart with more energy.

Workshop example: put team roles on Post-its to stick them on

TEAM CONFLICT

The interventions (Team Hi, Team Bye, Team Feedback, Team Roles) also serve to create a positive mood and atmosphere in the team to prevent possible team conflicts (ideally) or to create basis rituals for expressing and overcoming conflicts.

How conflicts affect the success of teamwork has a lot to do with their nature. Research distinguishes between three types of team conflict: relationship conflict, task conflict, and process conflict (Jehn, 1995). Not all conflict types have a negative impact on team results. Relationship conflicts (conflicts that arise at the relationship and personality level) as well as process conflicts (conflicts about the further procedure or the distribution of work) have been proven to have a negative influence on team results. Task conflicts, on the other hand, can either have a positive or negative effect on teamwork (Kurtzberg & Amabile, 2001).

Conflicts in teams are not only expectable and completely normal but, especially when aiming for a creative outcome, they are sometimes even necessary. Without any conflict, it will be difficult to come up with ideas and solutions that are as divergent (different) as possible. Too much harmony and the avoidance of conflicts can be harmful to creative teamwork. The main question is when and how often these conflicts occur and how the team manages them (Farh & Farh, 2010). For example, Tuckman's popular team-development model (1965) explicitly provides for an early, conflict-laden "storming" phase before the "performing" phase, with a "norming" phase in between. In "norming," existing rituals and a situation that offers psychological security can help groups take the leap (Fairchild & Hunter, 2014).

With regard to Design Thinking, opinion leaders' differences are often particularly noticeable in the divergent phases. These differences can be helpful to uncover fields of possibilities and make them as "broad" as possible (De Bono, 1970). However, they can also be a sign that the team has not yet reached a common understanding of the results of the last step, or they have a different understanding of the goal, or the phase of the project.

As previously mentioned, it helps to recognize task conflicts at an early stage, and use them as a resource. Otherwise, they can work themselves into the teamwork and cause relationship conflicts and process conflicts, with negative effects on project outcomes.

 Google study on "psychological safety": https://www.nytimes.com/2016/02/28/magazine/what-google-learned-from-its-quest-to-build-the-perfect-team.html

VI

SAMPLE AGENDAS

SAMPLE AGENDAS 1-DAY WORKSHOP

9:00	a.m.	→	Welcome and Warm-up
9:30	a.m.	→	Overview of Design Thinking
10:00	a.m.	→	Understand
10:30	a.m.	→	Observe
12:00	p.m.	→	Lunch
12:30	p.m.	→	Point of View I (Collecting, Storytelling, Clustering)
1:15	p.m.	→	Point of View II (persona, new question)

First understand the problem ...

2:00	p.m.	→	Ideate
2:30	p.m.	→	Prototype
3:30	p.m.	→	Break
3:45	p.m.	→	Present Results
4:15	p.m.	→	Define Next Steps
4:45	p.m.	→	I like, I wish
5:00	p.m.	→	End

Then solve the problem ...

SAMPLE AGENDAS 2-DAY WORKSHOP

DAY 1

9:00 a.m.	→	Welcome and Warm-up
9:30 a.m.	→	Overview of Design Thinking
10:00 a.m.	→	Understand
10:15 a.m.	→	Observe
12:45 p.m.	→	Lunch
1:45 p.m.	→	Define Point of View I (collecting, storytelling, clusters)
3:00 p.m.	→	Define Point of View II (persona, new question)
3:45 p.m.	→	Break
4:00 p.m.	→	Team Presentation of Day 1 Workshop-Results
4:45 p.m.	→	I like, I wish
5:00 p.m.	→	End

DAY 2

9:00 a.m.	→	Welcome and Warm-up
9:30 a.m.	→	Ideate
10:30 a.m.	→	Prototype
12:00 p.m.	→	Lunch
1:00 p.m.	→	Present team results, gather feedback
2:00 p.m.	→	Structure and implement feedback
3:00 p.m.	→	Define next steps
3:45 p.m.	→	Transfer project into working environment
4:15 p.m.	→	I like, I wish
4:30 p.m.	→	End

First understand the problem ...

Then solve the problem ...

VII

ABOUT THE AUTHORS

ABOUT THE AUTHORS

Isabell, Lena, and Inga met each other through their Design Thinking training and have been jointly moderating Design Thinking workshops since 2017.

© Anja Harnisch

DR. ISABELL OSANN

As a coach and consultant, Isabell Osann accompanies people and organizations in their continuous development. After completing her doctorate at the TU Berlin in the field of Organization & Management, Isabell joined KPMG, where she advised clients from a wide range of industries on change processes. Her transformation work included the integration of changing business requirements with new organizational structures or with IT, as well as necessary further employee development. Isabell expanded her consulting competencies through training in coaching and further education in the areas of communication, rhetoric, moderation and Design Thinking. After ten years of consulting, Isabell accepted the challenge of a visiting professorship in innovative teaching at Biberach University of Applied Sciences, where she established a cross-faculty Design Thinking Laboratory. At the same time, she dared to take the step into self-employment and founded "Kompetenz-aktivierung." Now she works with organizations on developing innovative solutions.

LENA MAYER

Lena Mayer conducts research at the Hasso Plattner Institute of the University of Potsdam on the topics of training, transfer in organizations, and (virtual) team collaboration. For her industrial doctorate, she is focusing on a case study at BASF. Together with her research team she develops and supervises massive open online courses (MOOC) on Design Thinking. So far, more than 18,000 learners signed up for their Design Thinking online courses worldwide. As an alumna of the HPI School of Design Thinking, she conducts workshops in an industrial and academic context.

Lena completed her master's degree in work and organizational psychology in Maastricht. Parallel to her studies, she founded the organization "Maastricht Disrupt" with fellow students. The group worked toward the goal of strengthening the user-centered design and interdisciplinary knowledge exchange in the region. In 2016 it organized the first Design Thinking Conference of the Maas-Rhine Euregio in the Cube Design Museum.

INGA WIELE

Inga Wiele is co-founder and managing director of the consulting firm "gezeitenraum" in St. Peter-Ording, which was named one of the best German business consultancies by the business magazine "brand eins" for the fifth time in 2019. Before that, she worked for many years as an SAP consultant in Germany and in the USA and as a product manager at SAP, where she was also a member of the supervisory board for two years.

During this time she has grown fond of the Design Thinking mindset. She appreciates it as a pragmatic standard for cooperation within various project teams while solving complex problems with high levels of uncertainty. The creative confidence she has gained through Design Thinking has inspired her to take the step into entrepreneurship with her husband. From the time she was trained at the Hasso-Plattner-Institut in Design Thinking (2011), she has also developed a passion for simple visualization. The majority of the drawings in this book are by her.

VIII REFERENCES

REFERENCES

Print

- Adenauer, J., & Petruschat, J. (2012): *Prototype! physical, virtual, hybrid, smart: tackling new challenges in design and engineering.* Berlin: form + zweck.

- Barker, L., & Watson, K. (2000): *Listen Up: How to Improve Relationships, Reduce Stress, and Be More Productive by Using the Power of Listening.* New York: St. Martin's Press.

- Csikszentmihalyi, M. (2015): Flow und Kreativität. 2. Auflage. Stuttgart: Klett-Cotta. (GER)

- Csikszentmihalyi, M. (2013): *Creativity: The Psychology of Discovery and Invention.* Harper Perennial Modern Classics.

- Curedale, R. (2013): *50 Brainstorming Methods: For team and individual ideation.* Topanga: Design Community College Inc.

- De Bono, E., & Zimbalist, E. (1970): *Lateral thinking* (pp. 1–32). London, UK: Penguin.

- Edmondson, A. (1999): Psychological safety and learning behavior in work teams. *Administrative science quarterly*, 44(2), pp. 350–383.

- Edmondson, A. C., & Harvey, J. F. (2018): Cross-boundary teaming for innovation: Integrating research on teams and knowledge in organizations. *Human Resource Management Review*, 28(4), pp. 347–360.

- Fairchild, J., & Hunter, S. T. (2014): "We've got creative differences": The effects of task conflict and participative safety on team creative performance. *Journal of Creative Behavior*, 48(1), pp. 64–87.

- Farh, J.-L., Lee, C., & Farh, C. I. C. (2010): Task conflict and team creativity: A question of how much and when. *Journal of Applied Psychology*, 95(6), pp. 1173–1180.

- Gumienny, R., Lindberg, T., & Meinel, C. (2011): Exploring the synthesis of information in design processes: opening the black-box. In DS 68-6: *Proceedings of the 18th International Conference on Engineering Design* (ICED 11), Impacting Society through Engineering Design, Vol. 6: Design Information and Knowledge, Lyngby/Copenhagen, Denmark, 15.–19.08. 2011.

- HPI-Stanford Design Thinking Research Program (2013): *Design Thinking Prototyping Cardset*. Potsdam: Hasso Plattner Institut für Softwaresystemtechnik.

- Jehn, K. A. (1995): A multimethod examination of the benefits and detriments of intragroup conflict. *Administrative science quarterly*, pp. 256–282.

- Klement, A. (2016): *When Coffee and Kale Compete*. New York: NYC Publishing.

- Kelley, T./Kelley, D. (2013): *Creative Confidence*. New York: Crown Business.

- Kolko, J. (2010): Abductive thinking and sensemaking: The drivers of design synthesis. *Design Issues*, 26(1), p. 17.

- Kolko, J. (2011): *Exposing the Magic of Design: A Practitioner's Guide to the Methods and Theory of Synthesis*. Oxford: Oxford University Press.

- Kurtzberg, T. R., & Amabile, T. M. (2001): From Guilford to creative synergy: Opening the black box of team-level creativity. *Creativity Research Journal*, 13(3-4), pp. 285–294.

- Lewrick, M., Link, P., & Leifer, L. (2017): *Das Design Thinking Playbook*. München: Vahlen. (GER)

- Liedtka, J. (2018): Why Design Thinking Works. *Harvard Business Review*, September-October issue: pp. 72–79.

- Menning, A., & Yasbay, M. (2015): The Idea Gym – training the design thinking muscle. Unpublished workshop guide.

- Menning, A., Beyhl, T., Giese, H., Nicolai, C., & Weinberg, U. (2014): Template-Based Documentation Support for Educational Design Thinking Projects. In *Proceedings of EPDE 2014*; International Conference on Engineering and Product Design Education.

- Mihaly Csikszentmihalyi (2013): *Creativity: The Psychology of Discovery and Invention* (Harper Perennial Modern Classics).

- Nichols, R. G., & Stevens, L. A. (1957): *Are you listening?* New York: McGraw-Hill.

- Ozenc, F. K., & Hagan, M. (2018): Ritual design: Crafting team rituals for meaningful organizational change. *Advances in Intelligent Systems and Computing*, 585, pp. 146–157.

- Robertson, A. (1994): *Listen for Success: A Guide to Effective Listening*. Burr Ridge: Irwin Professional Publishing.

- Smith, K. (2008): *How to Be an Explorer of the World: Portable Life Museum*. New York: Penguin Books.

- Šáchová-Kleisli, A., & Walther, B. (2015): Job-to-be-done-Logik in der Praxis. *Marketing Review St. Gallen*, 32(1). (GER)

- Tuckman, B. W. (1965): Developmental sequence in small groups. *Psychological bulletin*, 63(6), p. 384.

Digital

- Anderson et al. (2019): online course: Basics of Design Testing: https://open.sap.com/courses/ut1-2

- Brainstorming-Poster (n.d.): https://bit.ly/2Wj3ZOc (GER)

- Christensen, C. M. et al. (2016): Know Your Customers "Job to be Done." *Harvard Business Review*: https://hbr.org/2016/09/know-your-customers-jobs-to-be-done

- D-school Stanford, The K12 Lab Wiki (2014): Improv activities for Design Thinking: https://dschool-old.stanford.edu/groups/k12/wiki/3091c/Improv_activities_for_Design_Thinking.html

- Eckert, T. (2016): Was kreative Menschen gemeinsam haben. Ze.tt: http://ze.tt/was-kreative-menschen-gemeinsam-haben/ (GER)

- Gray, D. (2011): How-Now-Wow Matrix: https://gamestorming.com/how-now-wow-matrix/

- Gray, D. (2015): Draw Toast: https://gamestorming.com/draw-toast/

- Hasso Plattner Institut (n.d.): Warm-up Set, download: https://hpi-academy.de/fileadmin/hpi-academy/Infobroschüren/WarmUp-Set_deutsch_-_HPI_Academy.pdf (GER)

- HBR IdeaCast (2016): The "Jobs to be Done" Theory of Innovation. *Harvard Business Review*: https://hbr.org/ideacast/2016/12/the-jobs-to-be-done-theory-of-innovation

- I like I wish (n.d.): https://ilikeiwish.org/

- Improv Encyclopedia (n.d.): Warm-up: http://improvencyclopedia.org/categories//Warm-up.html

- Jobs-to-be-done (#JTBD) – Ein neuer Blick auf Kundenbedürfnisse (n.d.): https://digitaleneuordnung.de/blog/jobs-to-be-done/ (GER)

- Kegler, H. (2008): Ein Karren für alle. Deutsches Architektenblatt: https://www.dabonline.de/2008/02/01/ein-karren-fur-alle/ (GER)

- Kelley, D. (n.d.): untitled: http://www.designkit.org/mindsets

- Klement, A. (2013): Replacing The User Story With The Job Story: https://jtbd.info/replacing-the-user-story-with-the-job-story-af7cdee10c27

- Klement, A. (n.d.): Designing features using Job Stories: https://blog.intercom.com/using-job-stories-design-features-ui-ux/

- Liedtka, J. (2018): Why Design Thinking Works: https://hbr.org/2018/09/why-design-thinking-works

- Menning, A. (2015): LogCal – Template based documentation support. Hasso Plattner Institut – School of Design Thinking: www.logcal.de

- Rauch, J. (2009): Die Wissenschaft vom Musenkuss. Bild der Wissenschaft: https://www.wissenschaft.de/umwelt-natur/die-wissenschaft-vom-musenkuss/ (GER)

- Rozovsky, J. (2015): The five keys to a successful Google team. re:work: https://rework.withgoogle.com/blog/five-keys-to-a-successful-google-team/

- Taheri, von Schmieden & Mayer (2017): online course: Inspirations for Design: A Course on Human-Centered Design: https://open.hpi.de/courses/insights-2017

- The dribbblisation of design (n.d.): https://www.intercom.com/blog/the-dribbblisation-of-design/

- Understanding the Job (2016): https://www.youtube.com/watch?time_continue=77&v=sfGtw2C95Ms

- Video Arts (2017): John Cleese on Creativity in Management: https://www.youtube.com/watch?v=Pb5oIIPO62g

- Von Schmieden, Taheri & Mayer (2018): online course: Human-Centered Design: From Synthesis to Creative Ideas: https://open.hpi.de/courses/ideas2018

- Von Schmieden, Taheri & Mayer (2019): online course: Human-Centered Design: Building and Testing Prototypes: https://open.hpi.de/courses/prototype2019

- What Google Learned From Its Quest to Build the Perfect Team (2016): https://www.nytimes.com/2016/02/28/magazine/what-google-learned-from-its-quest-to-build-the-perfect-team.html

- 99U Local Dresden: Jan Schmiedgen (2015): https://vimeo.com/148199853

Quotes

- Isaac Newton in a letter to Robert Hooke, February 5, 1676; e.g. quoted in Chen, C. (2013): *Mapping Scientific Frontiers: The Quest for Knowledge Visualization*. London: Springer, p. 163.

- Lothar Zenetti in: Zenetti, L. (1972): *Texte der Zuversicht. Für den einzelnen und die Gemeinde*. München: Pfeiffer.

- Maya Angelou, quoted in: Kannings, A. (2014): *Maya Angelou: Her Words*. Morrisville: Lulu Press.

- Mark Miller (2012): https://thejanegroup.org/author/mark-miller/

- Sam Walton, quoted in: Bergdahl, M. (2010): *The 10 Rules of Sam Walton: Success Secrets for Remarkable Results*. Hoboken: John Wiley & Sons.

- Sara Blakely, quoted in: Kim, L. (August 26, 2014): 7 Insanely Rich Founders Share Their Best Business Advice. *Business Insider*: http://www.businessinsider.com/rich-entrepreneurs-best-business-advice-2014-8

DESIGN THINKING IN SIX PHASES

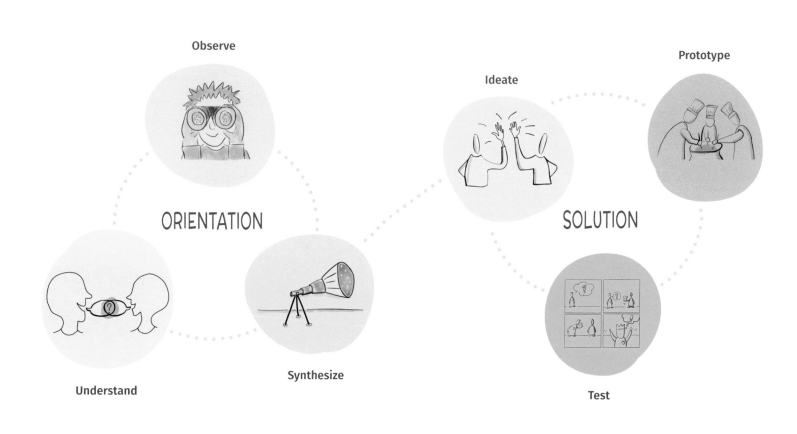

Observe

Ideate

Prototype

ORIENTATION

SOLUTION

Understand

Synthesize

Test

THANK YOU!

We received support from our families, friends, and colleagues while creating this book.
We would like to thank Dr. Mathias Osann, Prof. Dr. Verena Rath, Gina Meininger, Benedikt Ewald, Eugen Litwinow, Axel Menning, Prof. Dr. Boris Kühnle, Ines Mayer, Ida Mayer, and Bastien Grasnick.